BOTANICAL ART

AN IMAGE ARCHIVE FOR ARTISTS *And* DESIGNERS

INTRODUCTION

The art of botanical illustration has profoundly impacted artists and designers across different disciplines. Its precise observation of nature and emphasis on capturing intricate details have inspired countless artists to explore the natural world and incorporate botanical elements into their works. The accurate rendering of botanical subjects has influenced the field of scientific illustration, helping scientists communicate their research findings visually and accurately. Furthermore, botanical art has inspired designers in various industries, including fashion, textile, and interior design. The exquisite forms, patterns, and colours in botanical art have been translated into fabrics, wallpapers, and decorative motifs, bringing a touch of nature's beauty into everyday surroundings. Additionally, botanical art has influenced floral design, guiding florists in creating harmonious and aesthetically pleasing arrangements that celebrate the diversity of plant life. The delicate balance between scientific accuracy and artistic expression in botanical art continues to inspire and inform artists and designers, connecting the realms of art, science, and nature in a captivating way.

TABLE OF CONTENTS

BOTANICAL ART

DOWNLOAD YOUR FILES

Downloading your files is simple. To access your digital files, please go to the last page of this book and follow the instructions.

For technical assistance, please email:
info@vaulteditions.com

Bibliographical Note
This book is a new work created by Vault Editions Ltd.

ISBN:978-1-922966-15-5

VAULT EDITIONS

01
02
03
04
05
06

COMMON NAME: ROSE, SCIENTIFIC NAME: ROSA, FAMILY: ROSACEAE

07
08
09
10
11
12
13

COMMON NAME: ROSE, SCIENTIFIC NAME: ROSA, FAMILY: ROSACEAE

14
15
16
17
18
19
20

COMMON NAME: ROSE, SCIENTIFIC NAME: ROSA, FAMILY: ROSACEAE

21
22
23
24
25
26

COMMON NAME: ROSE, SCIENTIFIC NAME: ROSA, FAMILY: ROSACEAE

27
28
29
30
31
32
33

COMMON NAME: ROSE, SCIENTIFIC NAME: ROSA, FAMILY: ROSACEAE

34
35
36
37
38
39

COMMON NAME: ROSE, SCIENTIFIC NAME: ROSA, FAMILY: ROSACEAE

40
41
42
43
44
27
45

COMMON NAME: ROSE, SCIENTIFIC NAME: ROSA, FAMILY: ROSACEAE

46
47
48
49
50
51

COMMON NAME: ROSE, SCIENTIFIC NAME: ROSA, FAMILY: ROSACEAE

52
53
54
55
56
57

COMMON NAME: ROSE, SCIENTIFIC NAME: ROSA, FAMILY: ROSACEAE

58
59
60
61
62

COMMON NAME: CARNATION, SCIENTIFIC NAME: DIANTHUS CARYOPHYLLUS, FAMILY: CARYOPHYLLACEAE

63
64
65
66
67

COMMON NAME: CARNATION, SCIENTIFIC NAME: DIANTHUS CARYOPHYLLUS, FAMILY: CARYOPHYLLACEAE

68
69
70
71
72

COMMON NAME: CARNATION, SCIENTIFIC NAME: DIANTHUS CARYOPHYLLUS, FAMILY: CARYOPHYLLACEAE

73
74
75
76
77

COMMON NAME: CARNATION, SCIENTIFIC NAME: DIANTHUS CARYOPHYLLUS, FAMILY: CARYOPHYLLACEAE

78
79
80
81
82
83

COMMON NAME: CHRYSANTHEMUM, SCIENTIFIC NAME: CHRYSANTHEMUM, FAMILY: ASTERACEAE

84

85

86

87

COMMON NAME: CHRYSANTHEMUM, SCIENTIFIC NAME: CHRYSANTHEMUM, FAMILY: ASTERACEAE

88

89

90

91

COMMON NAME: CHRYSANTHEMUM, SCIENTIFIC NAME: CHRYSANTHEMUM, FAMILY: ASTERACEAE

92
93
94
95

COMMON NAME: COMMON DAISY, SCIENTIFIC NAME: BELLIS PERENNIS, FAMILY: ASTERACEAE

96
97
98
99

BOTANICAL ART

COMMON NAME: COMMON DAISY, SCIENTIFIC NAME: BELLIS PERENNIS, FAMILY: ASTERACEAE

100
101
102
103
104

COMMON NAME: COMMON DAISY, SCIENTIFIC NAME: BELLIS PERENNIS, FAMILY: ASTERACEAE

105
106
107
108

BOTANICALART

COMMON NAME: COMMON DAISY, SCIENTIFIC NAME: BELLIS PERENNIS, FAMILY: ASTERACEAE

109
110
111
112

COMMON NAME: COMMON DAISY, SCIENTIFIC NAME: BELLIS PERENNIS, FAMILY: ASTERACEAE

113

114

115

116

COMMON NAME: FREESIA, SCIENTIFIC NAME: FREESIA, FAMILY: IRIDACEAE

117

118

119

120

COMMON NAME: FREESIA, SCIENTIFIC NAME: FREESIA, FAMILY: IRIDACEAE

121

122

124

123

COMMON NAME: FREESIA, SCIENTIFIC NAME: FREESIA, FAMILY: IRIDACEAE

125
126
127
128
129
130

COMMON NAME: FREESIA, SCIENTIFIC NAME: FREESIA, FAMILY: IRIDACEAE

131
132
133
134
135

COMMON NAME: FREESIA, SCIENTIFIC NAME: FREESIA, FAMILY: IRIDACEAE

136
137
138
139

COMMON NAME: SUNFLOWER, SCIENTIFIC NAME: HELIANTHUS, FAMILY: ASTEROIDEAE

140
141
142
143

COMMON NAME: SUNFLOWER, SCIENTIFIC NAME: HELIANTHUS, FAMILY: ASTEROIDEAE

144

COMMON NAME: IRIS, SCIENTIFIC NAME: IRIS, FAMILY: IRIDACEAE

145

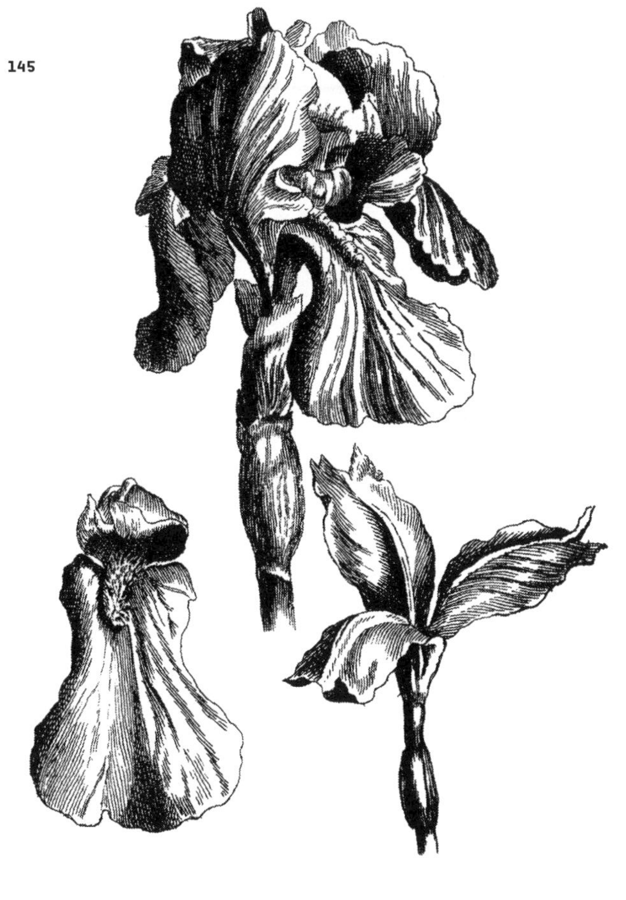

146

147

148

COMMON NAME: IRIS, SCIENTIFIC NAME: IRIS, FAMILY: IRIDACEAE

149
150
151
152

COMMON NAME: IRIS, SCIENTIFIC NAME: IRIS, FAMILY: IRIDACEAE

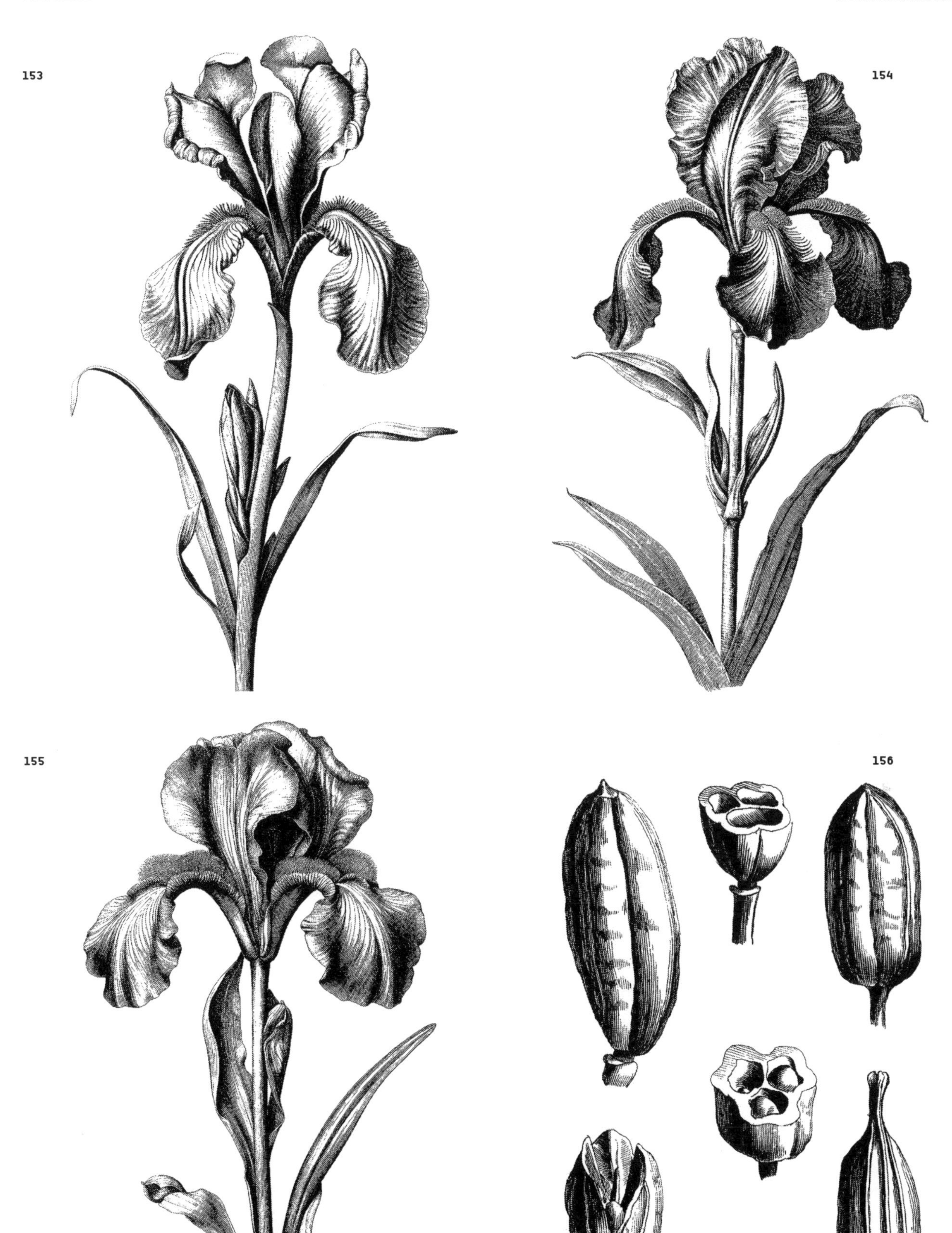
153
154
155
156

COMMON NAME: IRIS, SCIENTIFIC NAME: IRIS, FAMILY: IRIDACEAE

157
158

159
160

COMMON NAME: MARIGOLD, SCIENTIFIC NAME: TAGETES, FAMILY: ASTERACEAE

161
162
163
164
165

COMMON NAME: MARIGOLD, SCIENTIFIC NAME: TAGETES, FAMILY: ASTERACEAE

167
168
169
170
171

COMMON NAME: MARIGOLD, SCIENTIFIC NAME: TAGETES, FAMILY: ASTERACEAE

172
173
174
175

COMMON NAME: COMMON POPPY, SCIENTIFIC NAME: PAPAVER RHOEAS, FAMILY: PAPAVERACEAE

176
177
178
179

COMMON NAME: COMMON POPPY, SCIENTIFIC NAME: PAPAVER RHOEAS, FAMILY: PAPAVERACEAE

180
181
182
183
184
185

COMMON NAME: COMMON POPPY, SCIENTIFIC NAME: PAPAVER RHOEAS, FAMILY: PAPAVERACEAE

186
187
188
189
190

COMMON NAME: DAFFODIL, SCIENTIFIC NAME: NARCISSUS, FAMILY: AMARYLLIDACEAE

191
192
193
194

COMMON NAME: DAFFODIL, SCIENTIFIC NAME: NARCISSUS, FAMILY: AMARYLLIDACEAE

195

196

197

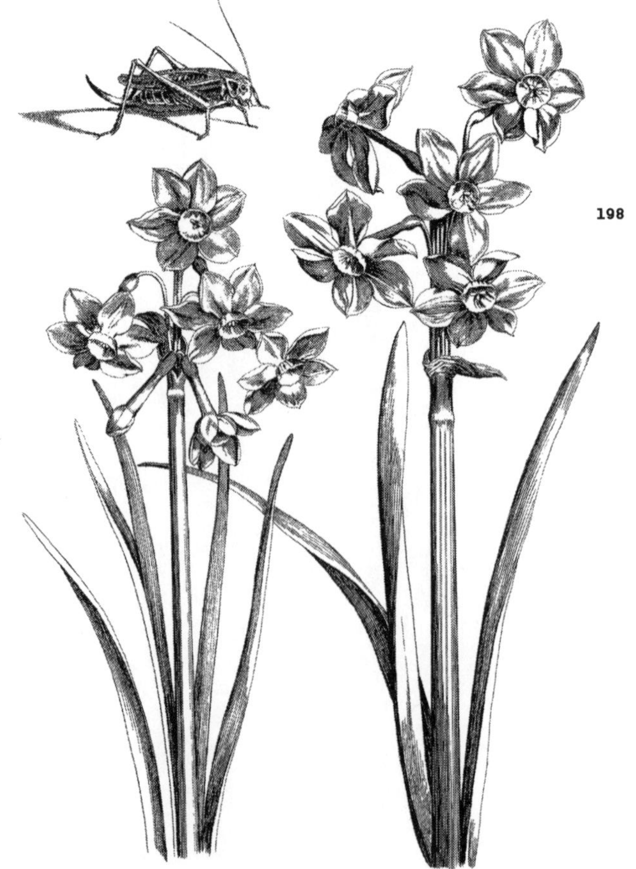

198

COMMON NAME: DAFFODIL, SCIENTIFIC NAME: NARCISSUS, FAMILY: AMARYLLIDACEAE

199
200
201
202
203
204

COMMON NAME: PEONY, SCIENTIFIC NAME: PAEONIA, FAMILY: PAEONIACEAE

205
206
207
208
209
210

COMMON NAME: PEONY, SCIENTIFIC NAME: PAEONIA, FAMILY: PAEONIACEAE

211
212
213
214
215
216

COMMON NAME: PEONY, SCIENTIFIC NAME: PAEONIA, FAMILY: PAEONIACEAE

217
218
219
220

COMMON NAME: TULIP, SCIENTIFIC NAME: TULIPA, FAMILY: LILIACEAE

221
222
223
224
225

COMMON NAME: TULIP, SCIENTIFIC NAME: TULIPA, FAMILY: LILIACEAE

226
227
228
229

COMMON NAME: TULIP, SCIENTIFIC NAME: TULIPA, FAMILY: LILIACEAE

230
231
232
233

COMMON NAME: TULIP, SCIENTIFIC NAME: TULIPA, FAMILY: LILIACEAE

234
235
236
237

COMMON NAME: ORCHID, SCIENTIFIC NAME: ORCHIDACEAE, FAMILY: ORCHIDACEAE

238

239

240

241

COMMON NAME: ORCHID, SCIENTIFIC NAME: ORCHIDACEAE, FAMILY: ORCHIDACEAE

242
243
244
245
246
247

COMMON NAME: DAHLIA, SCIENTIFIC NAME: DAHLIA, FAMILY: ASTERACEAE

248
249
250
251
252
253

COMMON NAME: DAHLIA, SCIENTIFIC NAME: DAHLIA, FAMILY: ASTERACEAE

254
255
256
257

COMMON NAME: DAHLIA, SCIENTIFIC NAME: DAHLIA, FAMILY: ASTERACEAE

258
259
260
261

COMMON NAME: LILY, SCIENTIFIC NAME: LILIUM, FAMILY: LILIACEAE

262
263
264
265
266

COMMON NAME: LILY, SCIENTIFIC NAME: LILIUM, FAMILY: LILIACEAE

267
268
269
270
271

COMMON NAME: LILY, SCIENTIFIC NAME: LILIUM, FAMILY: LILIACEAE

272
273
274
275
276
277

COMMON NAME: LOTUS, SCIENTIFIC NAME: NELUMBO NUCIFERA, FAMILY: NELUMBONACEAE

278
279
280
281

COMMON NAME: LOTUS, SCIENTIFIC NAME: NELUMBO NUCIFERA, FAMILY: NELUMBONACEAE

282
283
284
285
286
287

COMMON NAME: WATER LILY, SCIENTIFIC NAME: NYMPHAEACEAE, FAMILY: NELUMBONACEAE

288
289
290
291
292

COMMON NAME: WATER LILY, SCIENTIFIC NAME: NYMPHAEACEAE, FAMILY: NELUMBONACEAE

293

294

COMMON NAME: WATER LILY, SCIENTIFIC NAME: NYMPHAEACEAE, FAMILY: NELUMBONACEAE

295

296

COMMON NAME: WATER LILY, SCIENTIFIC NAME: NYMPHAEACEAE, FAMILY: NELUMBONACEAE

297
298
299
300
301

COMMON NAME: HIBISCUS, SCIENTIFIC NAME: HIBISCUS ROSA-SINENSIS, FAMILY: MALVACEAE

302
303
304
305
306
307

COMMON NAME: HIBISCUS, SCIENTIFIC NAME: HIBISCUS ROSA-SINENSIS, FAMILY: MALVACEAE

308
309
310
311
312
313
314
315

COMMON NAME: BIRD OF PARADISE, SCIENTIFIC NAME: STRELITZIA, FAMILY: STRELITZIACEAE

316
317
318
319
320

COMMON NAME: BIRD OF PARADISE, SCIENTIFIC NAME: STRELITZIA, FAMILY: STRELITZIACEAE

321
322
323
324
325

COMMON NAME: ANTHURIUM, SCIENTIFIC NAME: ANTHURIUM, FAMILY: ARACEAE

326
327
328
329

COMMON NAME: ANTHURIUM, SCIENTIFIC NAME: ANTHURIUM, FAMILY: ARACEAE

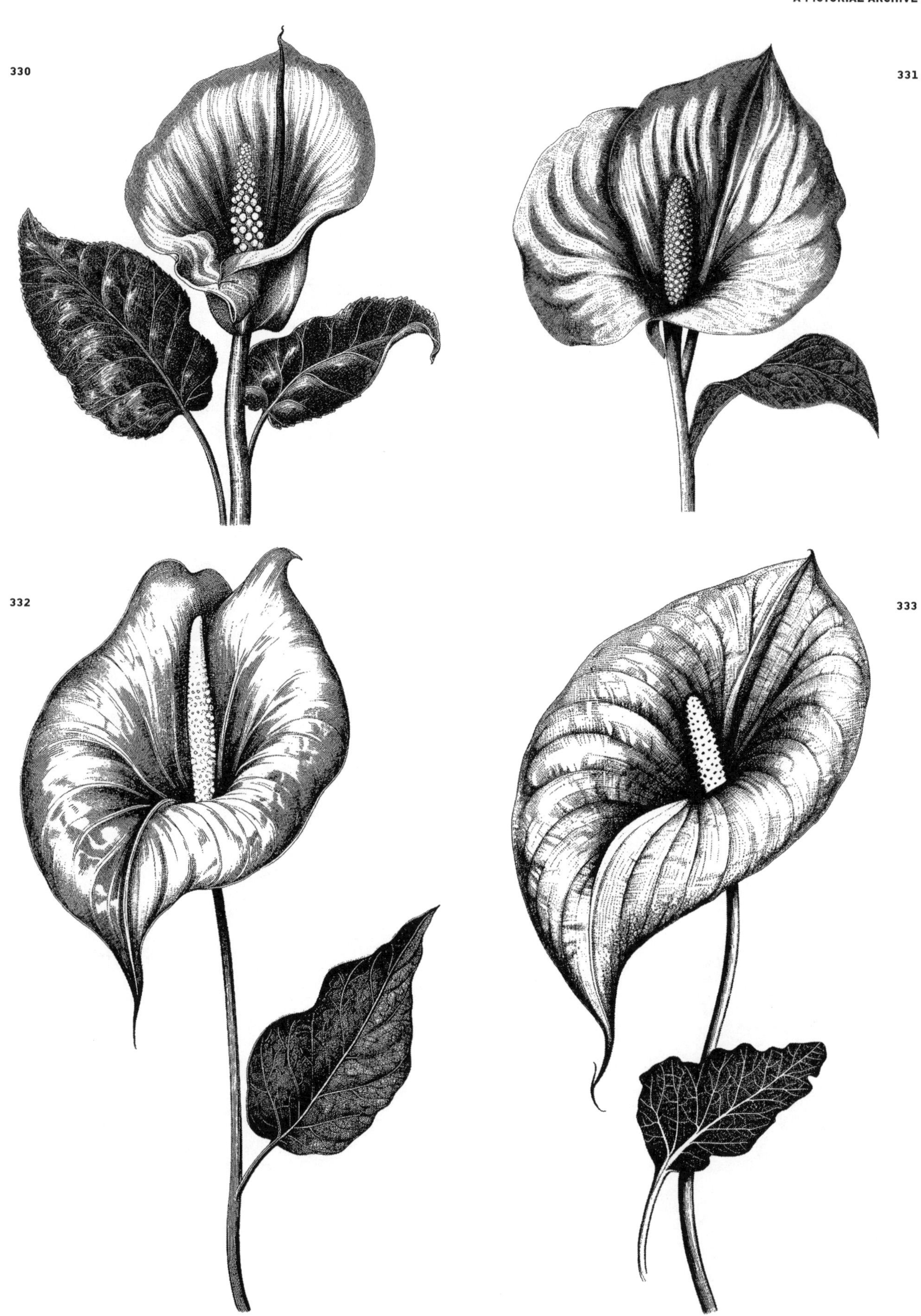
330
331
332
333

COMMON NAME: ANTHURIUM, SCIENTIFIC NAME: ANTHURIUM, FAMILY: ARACEAE

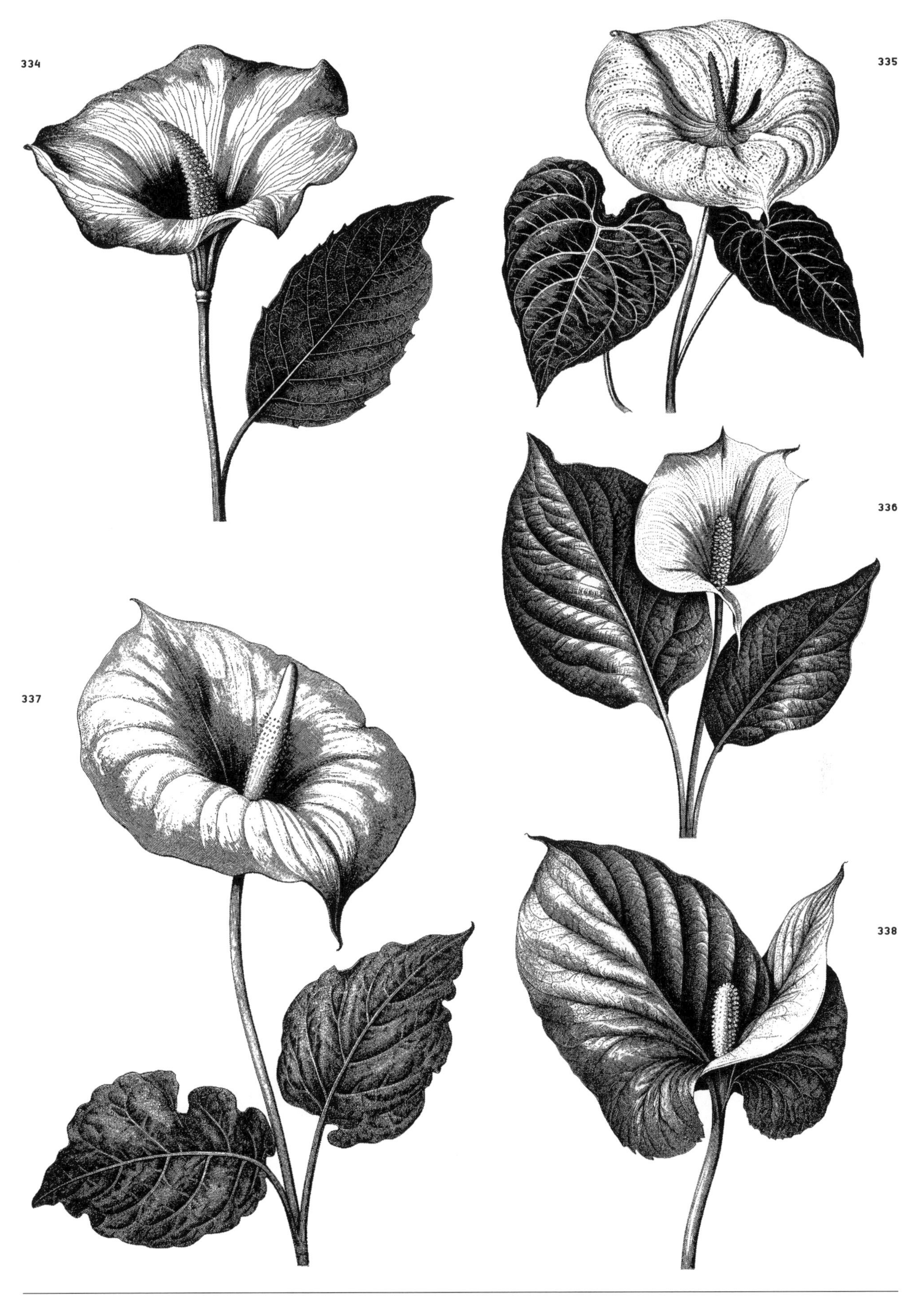
334
335
336
337
338

COMMON NAME: ANTHURIUM, SCIENTIFIC NAME: ANTHURIUM, FAMILY: ARACEAE

339
340
341
342

COMMON NAME: MONSTERA, SCIENTIFIC NAME: MONSTERA DELICIOSA, FAMILY: ARACEAE

343
344
345
346

COMMON NAME: MONSTERA, SCIENTIFIC NAME: MONSTERA DELICIOSA, FAMILY: ARACEAE

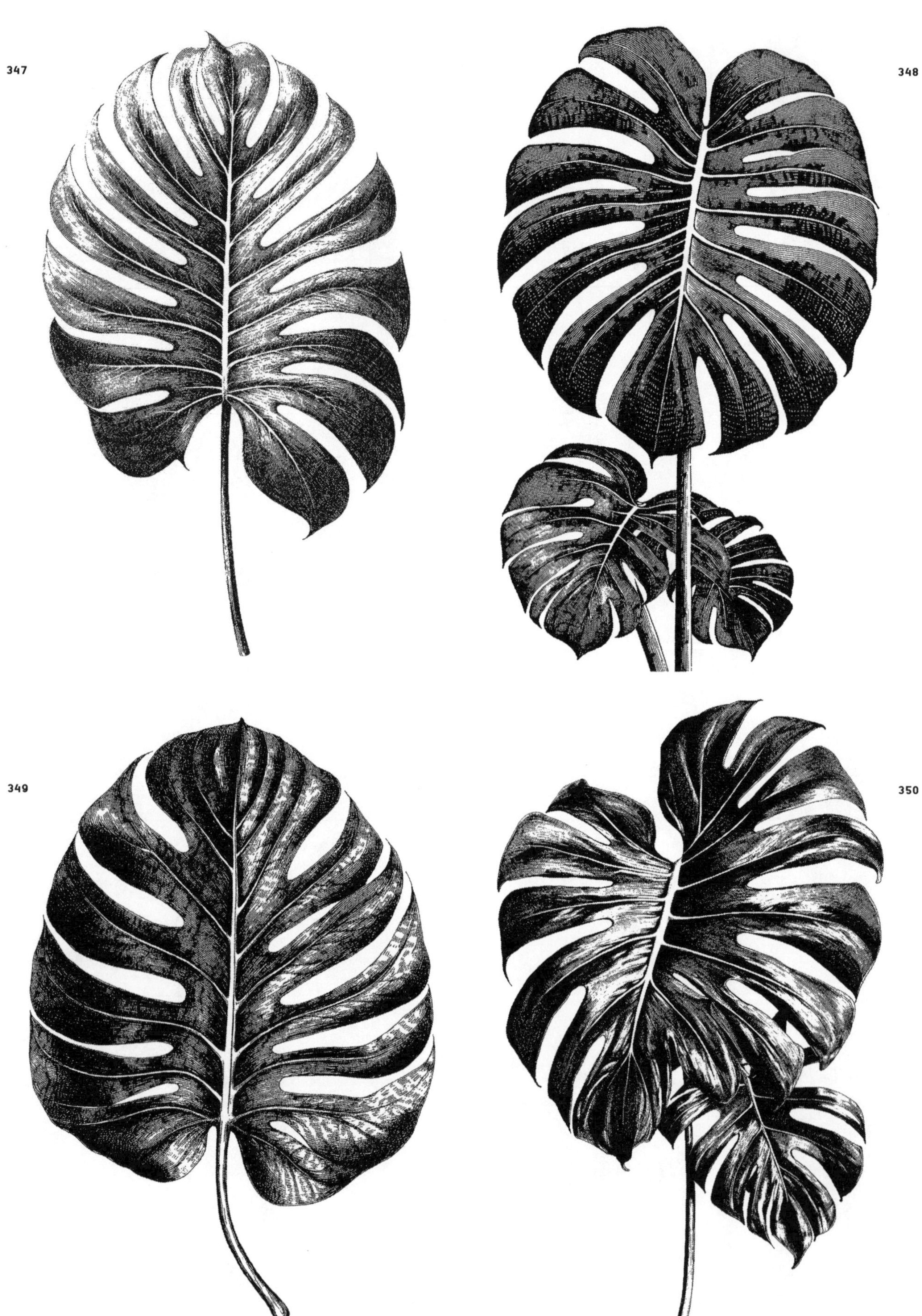
347
348
349
350

COMMON NAME: MONSTERA, SCIENTIFIC NAME: MONSTERA DELICIOSA, FAMILY: ARACEAE

351
352
353
354

COMMON NAME: MONSTERA, SCIENTIFIC NAME: MONSTERA DELICIOSA, FAMILY: ARACEAE

355
356
357
358
359

COMMON NAME: MONSTERA, SCIENTIFIC NAME: MONSTERA DELICIOSA, FAMILY: ARACEAE

360
361
362
363
364

COMMON NAME: SWORD FERN, SCIENTIFIC NAME: POLYSTICHUM MUNITUM, FAMILY: DRYOPTERIDACEAE

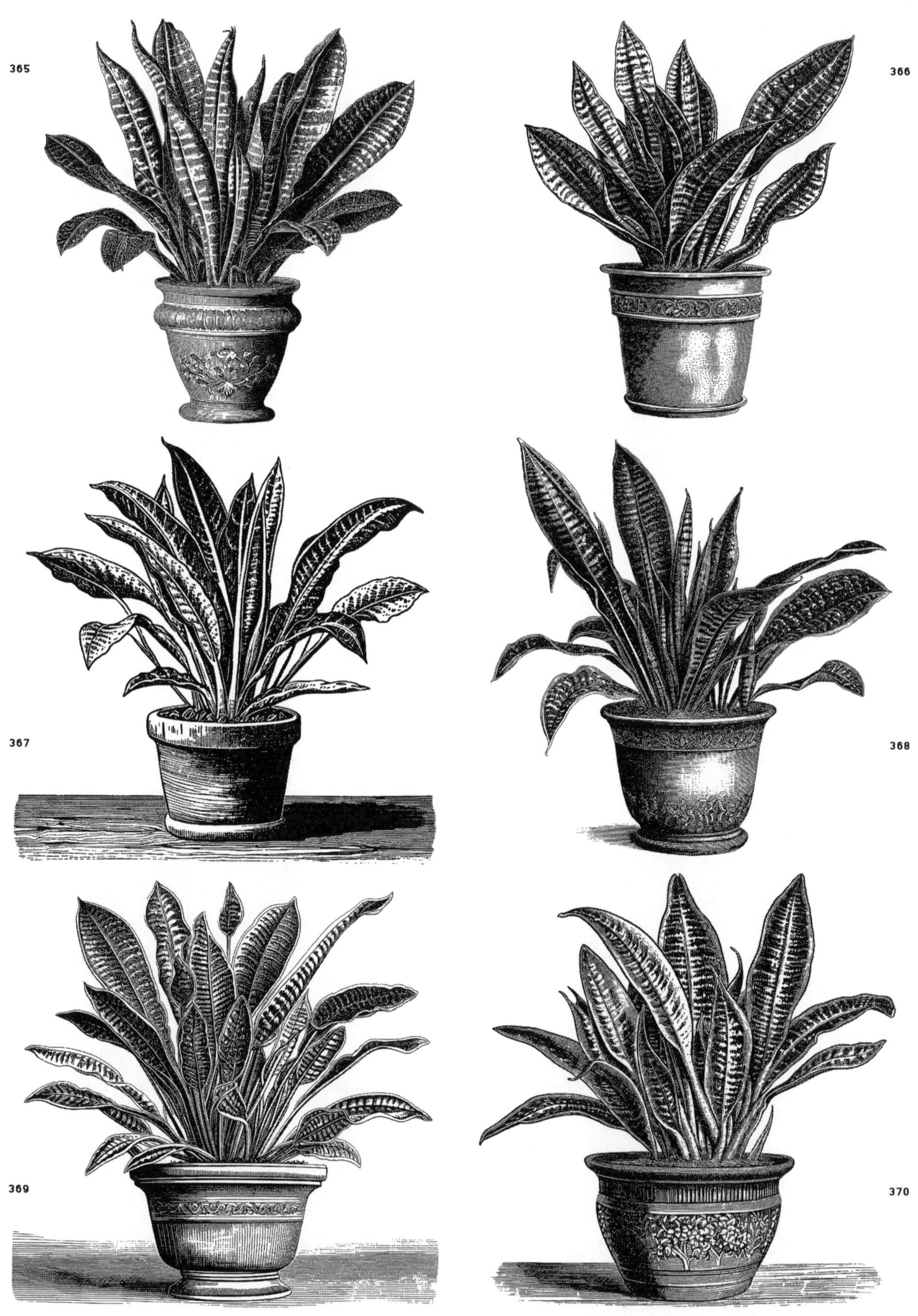
365
366
367
368
369
370

COMMON NAME: SNAKE PLANT, SCIENTIFIC NAME: DRACAENA TRIFASCIATA, FAMILY: ASPARAGACEAE

371

372

373

374

COMMON NAME: SNAKE PLANT, SCIENTIFIC NAME: DRACAENA TRIFASCIATA, FAMILY: ASPARAGACEAE

375
376
377
378
379

COMMON NAME: BIRD'S-NEST FERN, SCIENTIFIC NAME: ASPLENIUM NIDUS, FAMILY: ASPLENIACEAE

380
381
382
383

COMMON NAME: BIRD'S-NEST FERN, SCIENTIFIC NAME: ASPLENIUM NIDUS, FAMILY: ASPLENIACEAE

384

385

386

387

388

389

390

391

392

393

394

395

396

397

398

400

399

401

402

403

404

BOTANICAL ART

405

406

407

408

409

410

411

412

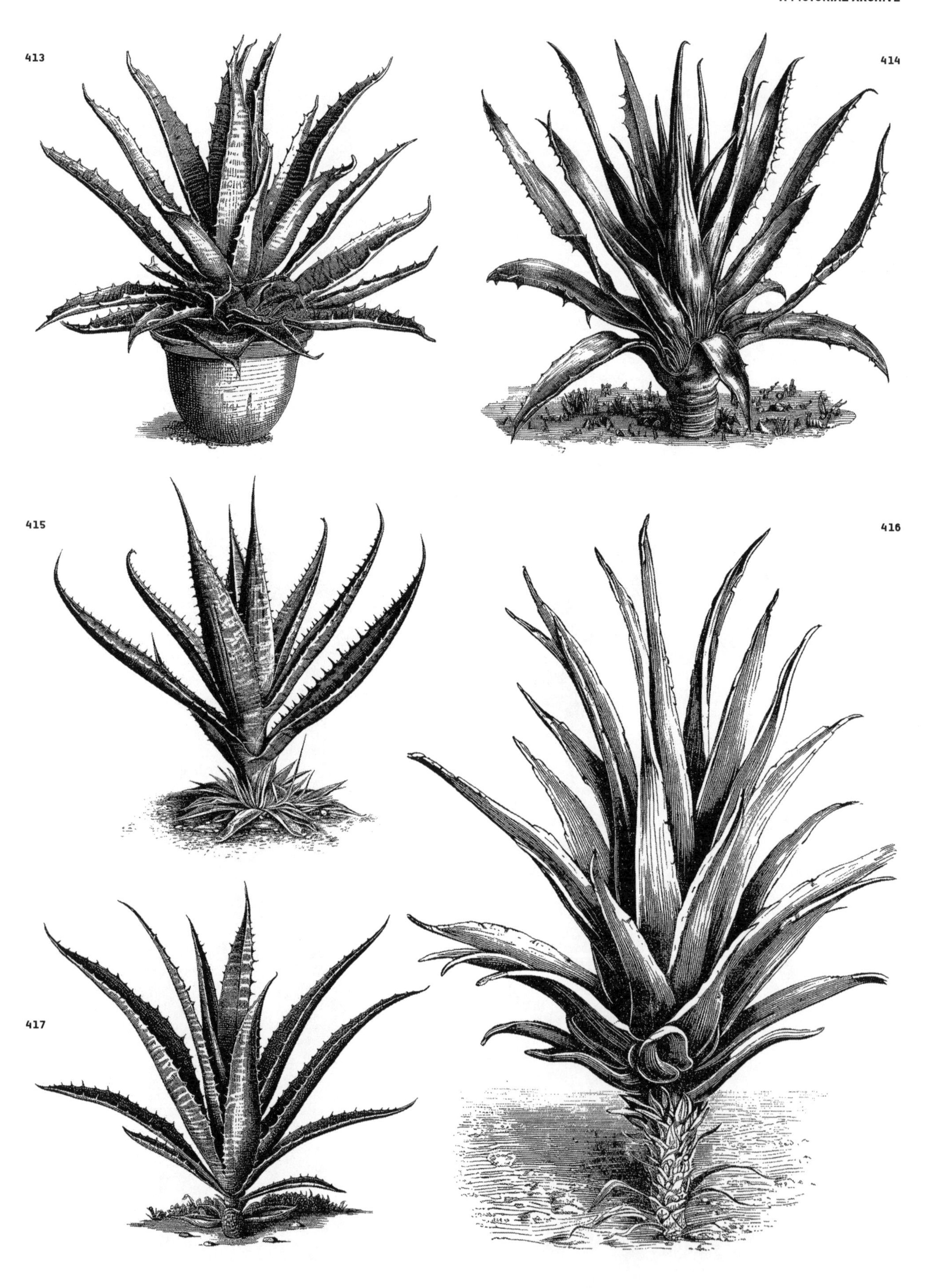
413
414
415
416
417

COMMON NAME: ALOE VERA, SCIENTIFIC NAME: ALOE VERA, FAMILY: ASPHODELACEAE

418

419

420

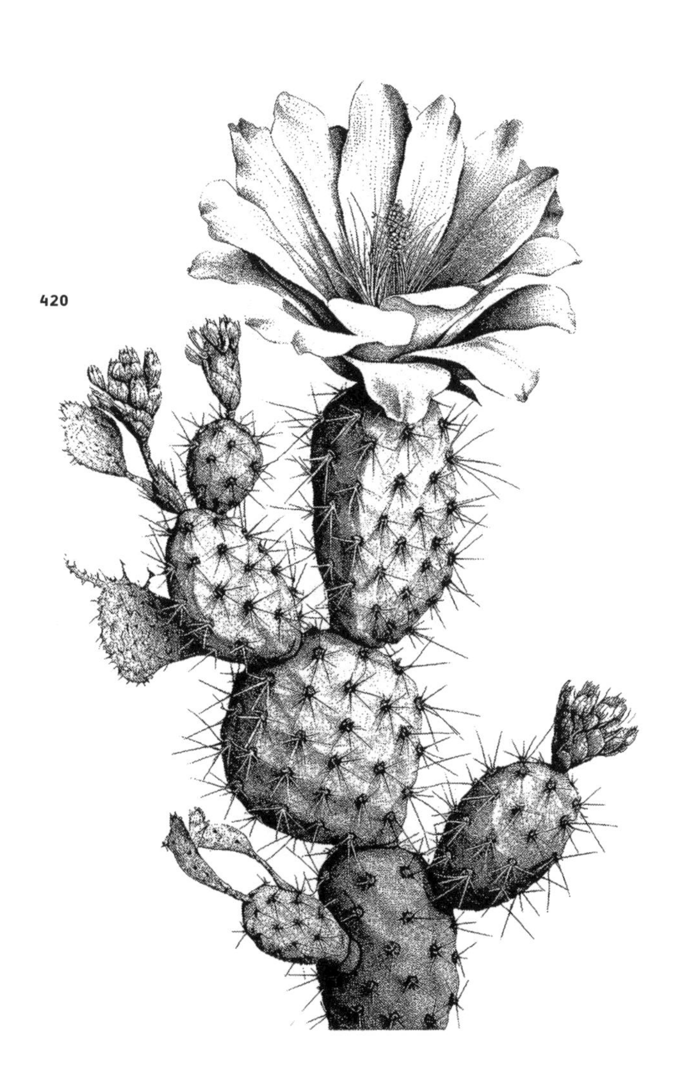

421

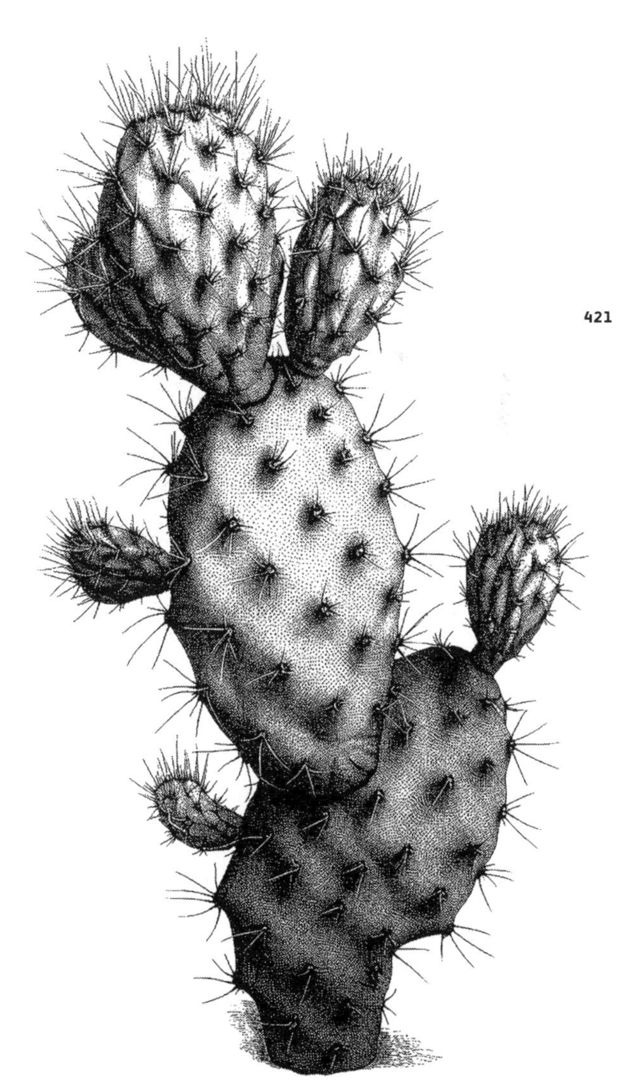

COMMON NAME: PRICKLY PEAR, SCIENTIFIC NAME: OPUNTIA, FAMILY: CACTACEAE

422

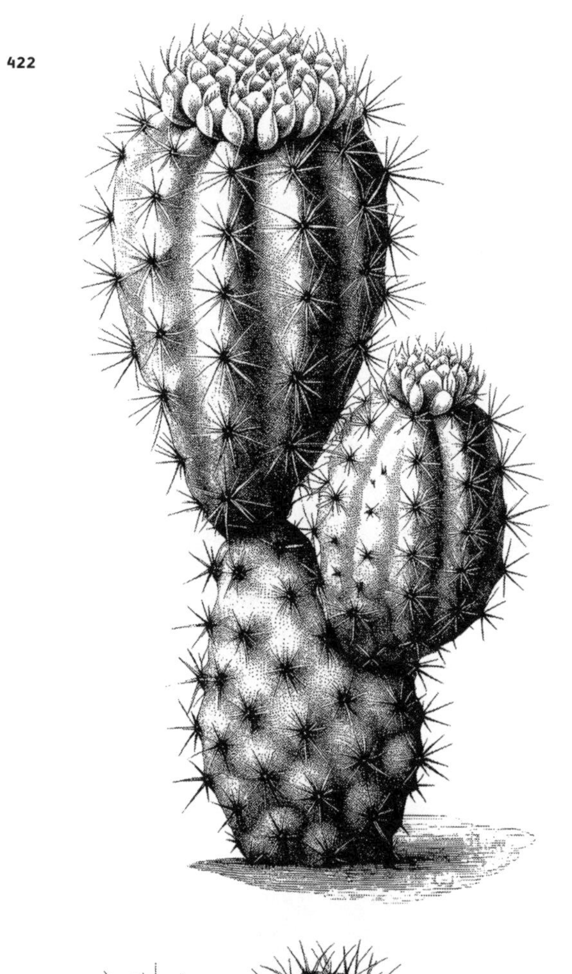

423

424

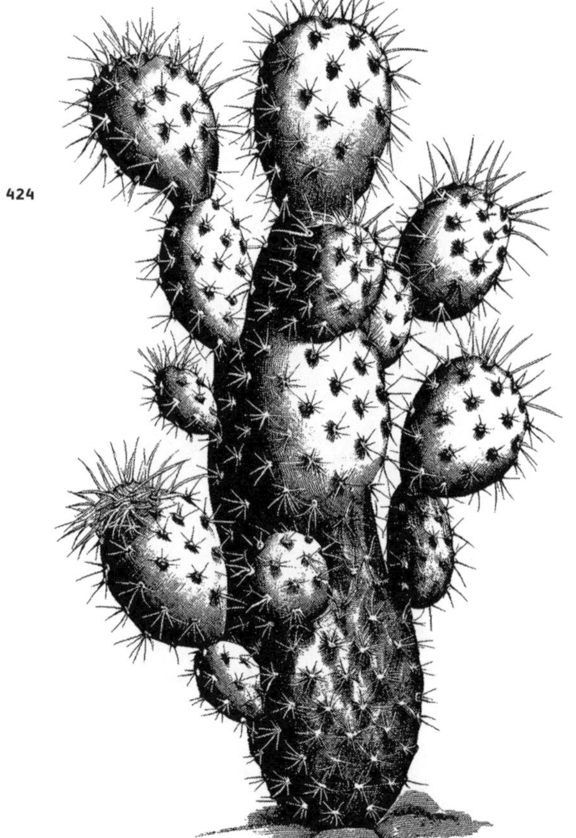

425

COMMON NAME: PRICKLY PEAR, SCIENTIFIC NAME: OPUNTIA, FAMILY: CACTACEAE

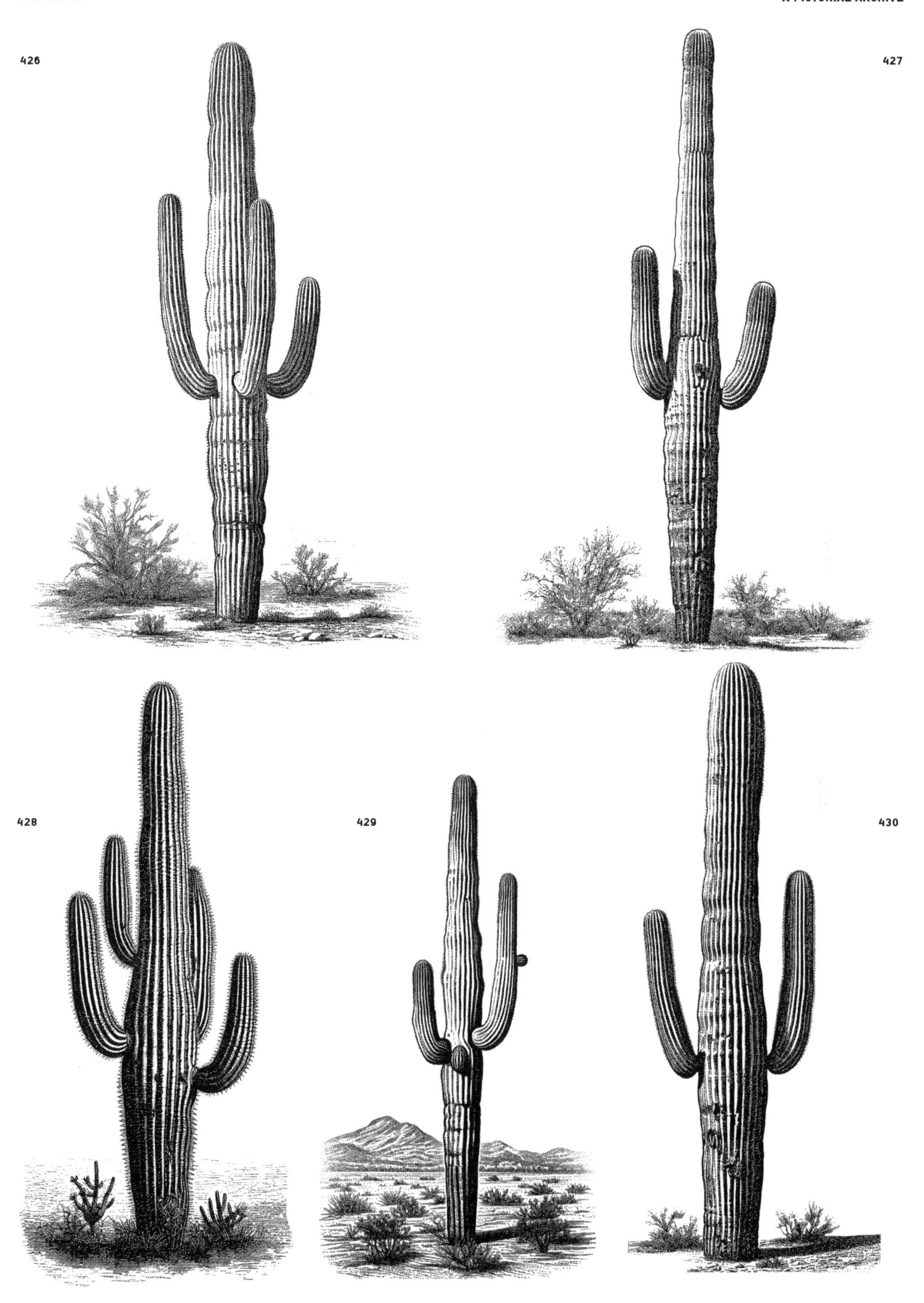
426
427
428
429
430

COMMON NAME: SAGUARO CACTUS, SCIENTIFIC NAME: CARNEGIEA GIGANTEA, FAMILY: CACTACEAE

431
432
433
434
435
436

COMMON NAME: GRASS, SCIENTIFIC NAME: POACEAE, FAMILY: POACEAE

437
438
439
440
441
442

COMMON NAME: GRASS, SCIENTIFIC NAME: POACEAE, FAMILY: POACEAE

443
444
445
446
447
448

COMMON NAME: GRASS, SCIENTIFIC NAME: POACEAE, FAMILY: POACEAE

449
450
451
452
453

COMMON NAME: GRASS, SCIENTIFIC NAME: POACEAE, FAMILY: POACEAE

454
455
456
457

COMMON NAME: GRASS, SCIENTIFIC NAME: POACEAE, FAMILY: POACEAE

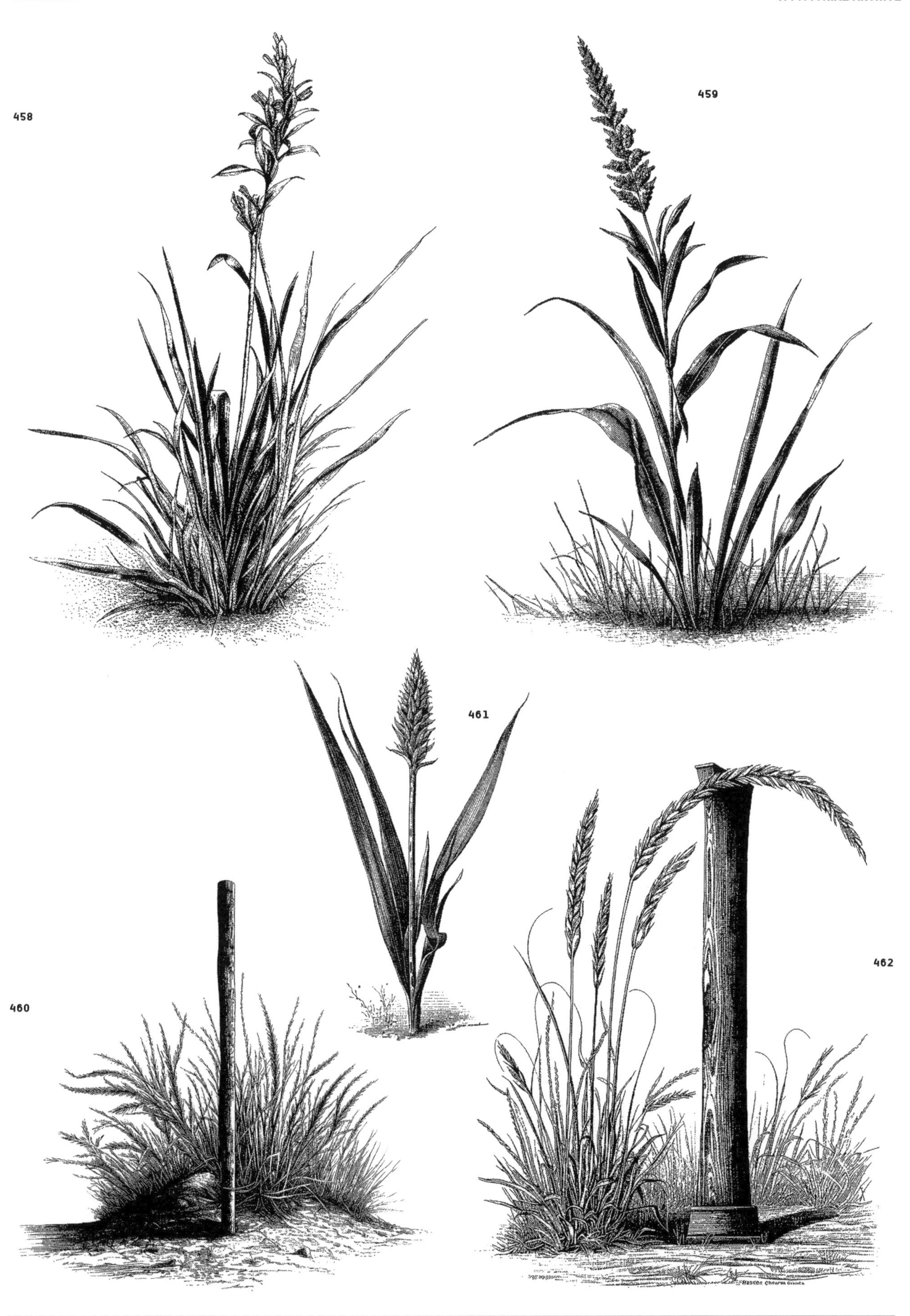
458
459
461
460
462

COMMON NAME: GRASS, SCIENTIFIC NAME: POACEAE, FAMILY: POACEAE

463
464
465
466
467

COMMON NAME: PINE TREE, SCIENTIFIC NAME: PINUS, FAMILY: PINACEAE

468
469
470
471
472

COMMON NAME: PINE TREE, SCIENTIFIC NAME: PINUS, FAMILY: PINACEAE

473

474

COMMON NAME: OAK, SCIENTIFIC NAME: QUERCUS, FAMILY: FAGACEAE

475

476

477

COMMON NAME: OAK, SCIENTIFIC NAME: QUERCUS, FAMILY: FAGACEAE

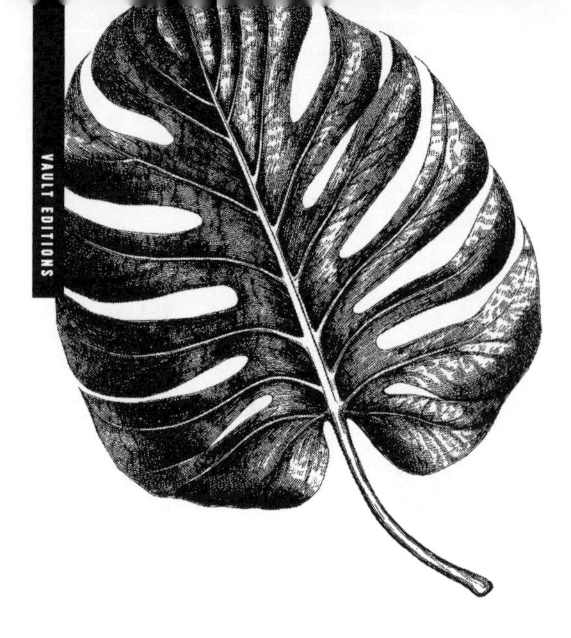
VAULT EDITIONS

VAULTEDITIONS.COM

LEARN MORE

At Vault Editions, our mission is to create the world's most diverse and comprehensive collection of image archives available for artists, designers and curious minds. If you have enjoyed this book, you can find more of our titles available at vaulteditions.com.

REVIEW THIS BOOK

As a small, family-owned independent publisher, reviews help spread the word about our work. We would be incredibly grateful if you could leave an honest review of this title wherever you purchased this book.

JOIN OUR COMMUNITY

Are you a creative and curious individual? If so, you will love our community on Instagram. Every day we share bizarre and beautiful artwork ranging from 17th and 18th-century natural history and scientific illustration, to mythical beasts, ornamental designs, anatomical illustration and more. Join our community of 100K+ people today—search @vault_editions on Instagram.

DOWNLOAD YOUR FILES

STEP ONE

Enter the following web address in your web browser on a desktop computer.

www.vaulteditions.com/pages/baa

STEP TWO

Enter the following unique password to access the download page.

bafap237346438sxda

STEP THREE

Follow the prompts to access your high-resolution files.

TECHNICAL ASSISTANCE

For all technical assistance, please email: info@vaulteditions.com

EDITIONS
Vault

Made in the USA
Las Vegas, NV
13 November 2024

11746555R00062